apartment **living**

ROCKPORT

GLOUCESTER MASSACHUSETTS

apartment living
New Designs for Urban Living

ROCKPORT PUBLISHERS

Margaret Crane   **Barbara B. Buchholz**

First published in the United States of America by

Rockport Publishers, Inc.

33 Commercial Street

Gloucester, Massachusetts 01930-5089

Telephone: (978) 282-9590

Facsimile: (978) 283-2742

www.rockpub.com

ISBN 1-56496-670-4

10 9 8 7 6 5 4 3 2 1

Design: Stephen Perfetto

Layout: SYP Design & Production

Cover Image: Fernando Bengoechea

Back Cover Image: Peter Margonelli

Printed in China.

Introduction

The apartment, like the martini, swing dancing, and the Volkswagen Beetle, has come back in style, but not as the abode of yesteryear. It is a contemporary domicile—not just an apartment, but, as is now the preferred term, an "apartment home."

The variety of apartment homes is extensive, with styles that have evolved over time. There are the familiar high-rise apartments, which were built initially for the wealthy who lived in cities and preferred the security and views that came with living up high. Eventually, this style of apartment housing spread to the suburbs. The architecture of many of these early high-rise structures reflected the legacy and designs of famous early architects such as Louis Sullivan and Walter Gropius.

Later came low-lying garden apartment complexes that had to their advantage expanses of coveted outdoor space. These designs, both in the city and suburbs, often have footpaths and badminton courts, landscaped swimming pools, fitness centers, volleyball courts, security staff, concierge service, automated or remote-control features, and other electronic conveniences.

Lofts soon followed, which differ aesthetically from other types of apartments. These were carved out of empty industrial buildings because of the immense space, openness, light, and affordability they offered die-hard urbanites who often wanted to work where they lived and needed the space to spread out the tools and furnishings of their trade. As this style of apartment has become more accepted and mainstream, it has been copied with chic lofts built from scratch in the suburbs and outlying city areas.

Along with apartment homes' greater diversity and new nomenclature comes heightened responsibility. The spaces in these apartments-cum-houses are expected to function like homes with full amenities and storage, not to mention efficiency and comfort.

But whether they are large or small, old or new, apartments still need to be filled with certain old-fashioned commodities, such as charm and grace, and an owner's sense of style. The apartment provides the backdrop, but the resident needs to stage his or her own production, playing up the space's strengths and downplaying any weaknesses.

The apartment dweller need no longer feel confined by low-ceilinged, shoe-box-shaped apartments that do not lend themselves to a fancy or old-world feeling. Tricks of the trade can help mold any configuration to fit nearly any desire. Furnishings and decorations can be edited to create more white space or to cleverly display favorite possessions and collections in tiny domiciles. In larger abodes, a sense of crowded opulence or generous spartan space can be achieved through a few grand gestures.

For many years, the primary apartment decision was whether to rent or to buy, but that, too, is changing. Historically, if the decision was to buy it meant finding a cooperative. The building's cooperative association owned the entire structure, including the individual units and the common spaces of hallways, lobbies and any garage or outdoor space; owners purchased shares or a percentage ownership in the building. How many shares they gained versus a neighbor depended on the sizes of their apartment units. Another type of apartment ownership emerged later—the condominium. In this setup, owners bought their units, along with a part of the common areas.

Decorating an apartment—whatever style, size, or type—takes a special eye and careful consideration of lifestyle. Fortunately, it does not all have to be decorated in a flash; months and, yes, years can go by before the decor is complete. There is great pleasure in decorating an apartment slowly, sort of like savoring a wonderful book. You can decorate as you go with a little nip here, a little tuck there when you have the urge, the time, and the money.

Challenges will abound, depending on whether the apartment is meant to be a crash pad or pied-a-terre—a city home away from home. Its use needs to be taken into account. Is it your primary residence, a workspace, a refuge, an all-purpose family place, or a first apartment—one you'll always cherish, like a first kiss. If it is a temporary home or a rental, for example, it may not warrant major renovations.

Since many apartments in cities are small, a major challenge is making them look larger and cleaner. On the flip side, decorating when space is not at a premium can also be tough as it can be difficult to make the enormous square footage feel intimate and on a human scale. Still other problems need to be tackled: working with existing architectural elements such as columns, archways, and doorways; making do with minuscule kitchens or oversized entry halls; becoming creative with limited storage, shared hallways, and narrow, high-up balconies, and roofdecks.

There is a long list of what we dream of having in our apartments, which reflects the amenities of the suburban home and neighborhood. We want apartments to look like comfortable houses with all the anticipated rooms, appliances, and details. We also want them to be fully up-to-date and have proper electrical connections for our state-of-the-art appliances and computer equipment, space for utility equipment, snazzy bathrooms and kitchens, and well-outfitted closets.

The apartment home can become a colorful collage of all these requirements and one where the pieces fit tidily together like a well-completed jigsaw puzzle. It is up to you to plan, decorate, and hammer away—or hire someone to help you do so. When done, you can stretch out on that chaise on your terrace or in your bedroom, with a cold glass of lemonade or a hot cup of tea, and enjoy your accomplishments and new surroundings.

—Barbara B. Buchholz and Margaret Crane

smaller *is* better

LESS CAN OFTEN BE MORE, and if you live in a small space, whether a one-room studio or a slightly larger pied-a-terre, it can be helpful to take a minimalist approach to its design. But do not think of the challenge as giving up and doing without. The good news is that small offers many advantages since you do not have to buy and arrange as many furnishings and accessories, and you do not have to spend as much time taking care of them. Furthermore, living in small spaces is an increasingly popular choice among people of all walks and stages of life. These include busy business executives who are eager to find and establish temporary crash pads after an exhausting day at work; countless young people who have just graduated from college and are without an excess amount of time, money, and home-furnishing ideas; and empty nesters who are seeking to downsize, knowing that bigger is not necessarily best at every stage of their lives.

In each case, although the impetus may be different, the requirements are the same: you need to have enough comforts to create a real home, but you want to be careful not to accumulate so many comforts as to make the space feel and look crowded and even smaller. Each of the primary groups who tend to choose scaled-down square footage, and their unique challenges and preferences are detailed in this chapter.

Student and Young-Professional Digs

When money is at a premium, priorities have to be established. It is smartest to invest in good, long-term essentials that can travel later to larger quarters: a well-made sofa, a dining table, end tables, some chairs, a bed, and cooking and serving equipment. If quarters consist of just one big room that combines the functions of eating, cooking, sleeping, sitting, and reading, keep furnishings small scale and not too quirky. Pieces that later might look too small in a larger home can always be recycled into more casual, smaller rooms, such as a library or family room, or from the master bedroom or sitting room into a child's bedroom. You may also want to physically divide some spaces in a small apartment with screens or dividers or a tall piece of furniture, such as a high chest of drawers. A corner of a living room can be cordoned off to offer some privacy for a desk in an at-home office, or a low row of chests can separate two beds when roommates share a bedroom.

(above) Hang a wooden rack behind a door to hold hats, bags, and other accessories to create a clean looking, workable space in a small apartment. These items stay hidden from view when the door is closed, but when it's ajar, the objects become a cleverly crafted sculpture that is a perfect blend of artistry and function.

(left) Dining and creative design coexist in this snug South Beach, Florida, love nest apartment. A dance of patterns, and parallel and perpendicular lines define this room. A white-on-white tablecloth with a wave pattern, heart-shaped backs on cane chairs, and a playful gallery of postcards strung across two clotheslines come together to create a whimsical display. A silver, multistar-shaped ceiling fixture provides light.

Pieds-a-Terre

As the world has changed, so has the way we live. The new global economy now gives cities, suburbs, towns, and even rural areas a heightened role to play in daily lives. With no place completely out of bounds, an increased number of residents seek temporary accommodation for pleasure and business in far-flung locales. A hotel can sometimes be too impersonal, expensive, or hard to secure on a regular basis; similarly, a friend or family member's offer of a place to stay wears thin after repeated visits. On the other hand, a pied-a-terre, which translates from the French to a "foot on the ground," offers an appealing alternative as a little home away from home. In such abodes, owners can hang their hat (literally), stretch out, and really relax, surrounded by a few cherished furnishings and mementos. Think of the space in the same vein as a Bach cantata—short and sweet, rather than a full symphony played by an orchestra. These small, second homes-away-from-home present a refuge from the commotion of a day's work or play, and a platform to jump back into the world after rest and refreshment. They become a place to slip into something comfortable and familiar, enjoy breakfast casually, chat or work on the phone, and stash needed belongings and supplies for the next visit.

Because these spaces are not used all the time and are typically small, you do not need to spend a lot on the furnishings. Invest in some good-quality primary pieces such as a comfortable sofa and bed, an expandable dining table that can double as a desk with appropriate chairs, maybe an area rug or two, an end table and coffee table, and a few favorite accents to add warmth and personality. You might also include a beloved art piece or two, some cherished books, and a favorite inexpensive collection such as snowglobes, fish decoys, postcards, or family photos to further the feeling of home.

(left) This plain vanilla bathroom has become a most important and pleasing room and is as comfortable as an old pair of jeans. An aquatic theme predominates, visible in the starfish that line the arch above the curtained shower-tub combination. A small mirror placed above the vintage sink expands the small space.

(opposite) Dedicate a spot in your apartment to showcase a favorite theme. No matter how small a space is, there is always room for a little ingenuity. In this seaside living room, a non-working fireplace houses a collection of seashells and starfish, expressing the inhabitants' love of the shore. Candles create a sense of romance. The mirror over the fireplace gives the illusion of more space to the small room.

Empty Nester Retreats

After years of accumulating possessions, it is difficult to simplify and pare down. However, it is essential when going from a large number of rooms down to just a few. How is this accomplished? Slowly. Before moving in, add up the new square footage, draw up a plan and sketch in your favorite furnishings that you do not want to let go of. Do not throw or give away question-marked items forever; instead, bequeath them to a friend or family member (with the understanding you may ask for them back) so that you can retrieve them if you find an extra nook or corner. You can put other items that you are not sure what to do with in storage until the new space is arranged and tested. Finally, those pieces that you have absolutely no use for but that are still in good condition, can be given away or donated to a charity.

(left) Ornamentation serves a practical purpose in this jewel box of a kitchen. The butterfly and fish magnets decorating the refrigerator door project the owners' chic sense of style. These travel mementos add coziness to the room and provide an instant visual scrapbook of the owners' lives and loves. The aquatic theme is carried throughout in starfish and other bric-a-brac and beyond in the rest of the apartment.

(opposite) Living in a small apartment does not mean scaling back to the purely practical. This canopy treatment crowns the bed below it and also performs an optical illusion by making the ceiling appear higher. A red-and-white striped wing chair and canary yellow walls provide colorful counterpoints.

...add up the new square footage, draw up a plan and sketch in your favorite funishings.

(opposite) clockwise from top left:
A powerful play of lines and space creates architectural interest in a tight area. Here, a stunning wood-slat spiral staircase when juxtaposed against a living room's plain geometry becomes a sculpture. The red window treatment adds drama.

Choose furnishings carefully for small rooms. In this space, a wood sofa does double duty and changes the purpose of the room with whatever manifestation it takes on. When the sofa is strewn with cushions, it becomes a comfortable spot to relax in the living room. Add more cushions to the floor for a cozy conversation area. Or, take the cushions off, pull up one of those stacked chairs in the corner, and use the sofa as a desk. Voila! You have a home office.

A filing cabinet holding important documents was placed next to the sofa in the same room. A lamp on top of the filing cabinet transforms the piece into an end table when it's time to turn the space back into a living room.

In this cozy space, the wood Parson's bench is pulled out from the wall to double as a table for dining, working, or entertaining. The uncarpeted hardwood floor provides a stage for a collection of sculptures, lamps and objects d'art in various sizes and shapes. A milk glass floor lamp provides soft illumination.

Bringing It All Together

To fashion a smaller apartment into a livable, homey space requires skill. Many experienced designers know that the best design idea is, again, to plan. Begin with a rough floor plan and color scheme, then fill in slowly. To get the most out of your space, use furniture of mixed proportions, some three-dimensional art, a large mirror, and good lighting through a variety of table and wall lamps, ceiling fixtures, and wall sconces. Compact appliances, such as stackable washers and dryers, under-the-counter refrigerators, and small corner sinks, all help to preserve space and give the illusion of more room.

Many rooms can also be designed to serve more than one function. A dining room or alcove might double as a guest room with a screen separating the sitting and sleeping areas. A futon in the living room might serve as a chair or couch during the day and a place to sleep at night, leaving the bedroom to become an office or studio. Pocket and accordion doors can cordon off a hall or entry, so it can double as extra storage or hanging space. Movable furniture on casters—a fully outfitted office with space for a computer, fax machine, and phone—can go where it is needed, including being placed out of view in a closet or other room when clients or company arrive.

Finally, gain additional room by taking full advantage of vertical spaces. Build shelves above doorways, around the perimeter of ceilings, and underneath windows that do not extend to the ground. Remember, whatever type of small apartment is selected, even small spaces need a bit of drama or whimsy to come alive. Consider a few elaborate fabrics or draperies, several fanciful paintings, a great paint treatment, a grouping of unusual knickknacks, or any decorative show stopper that grabs the eye. However you outfit your space, the ultimate goal should be the same: to have a home that allows you to live as comfortably and effortlessly as possible.

Make the most of every nook, cranny, andÖvista? Function took precedence over the view in this diminutive domicile. A 1920s chinoiserie desk with ebony-colored bent wood chair and black-and-white mock Chinese lamp pushed against the window set the stage for a work space with appeal and practicality.

An exotic flavor dominates this cozy living room/den. The leopard-print sofa, a 1940s coral-colored chinoiserie coffee table and plush armchairs covered in a multicolored Oriental print complete the theme. Bronze candlesticks sit atop the coffee table, tying the room together as well as providing a light source for intimate gatherings.

(previous page) A small room has the illusion
of grandeur and whimsy thanks to a few
careful and eclectic touches. The walls were
upholstered in a hand-blocked Indian cotton,
creating an elegant backdrop for a couple
of silk button-tufted Victorian chairs, a
Fortuny hanging lamp, and cotton candy
pink lily-pad tables.

(opposite) Color and pattern plays a major
role when creating a sense of drama in a
small space. Here, the sofa was covered in
a stunning black-and-white hand-blocked
print, which is complemented by subtle
dabs of color expressed in the wallpaper
and delightful pink irises.

(above) Fool the eye by making a room look bigger than it actually is. One technique is to give the illusion of a large, continuous space. In this room, the drapes were made in an identical color and pattern as the wallpaper to achieve that effect.

(opposite) Strip a snug space to the bones and bring it back to life through dramatic design. This guest bedroom in a Manhattan apartment is exotic and bold, from its sensational Chinese red lacquered walls to the stenciled purple Siberian irises surrounding the cast-iron daybed.

apartmentalize

Small-Scale Style

When space is at a premium, rooms and furnishings should reflect the same ambience and be less ornate and complicated. But do not just do without. Try adding moldings between the walls and ceiling. Moldings can reduce the amount of flat ceiling your eye perceives, which makes a room seem taller and, hence, more grand. Let your creative energy flow by making your apartment a place of accumulated, yet pared, charm.

A *flea-market footstool* can become a very respectable coffee or side table with the right collection of books or magazines on top.

Line up a *stack of books* horizontally atop a pine carpenter's bench or vertically on a chest or round table for some high-brow charm. Attach tables or chairs to walls, as the Shakers used to do, to create the illusion they are levitating. This opens up your space and extends the eye visually toward the center of the room.

Use *mirrors and glass* to expand a small space, either sparingly or in a big way. Cover an entire door or wall in an entry hall or let a mirror be the focal point of a room—above a fireplace, for example. To subtly encourage a sense of spaciousness, light a living room or bedroom with clear-glass table lamps, or adorn a dining room table with a collection of clear- glass vases.

(above) Shelving gives order to this pied-a-terre bedroom-cum-library. Books are neat and accessible. Although the shelves look like built-ins, they can actually be put on casters and moved to another section of the space. A tall gold leaf mirror makes the high-ceilinged room seem larger than it is.

(opposite) Make sure only one piece of furniture dominates a pint-sized room. An inviting bed takes over a corner of this apartment to create a sleeping nook. Covered with a plush down comforter in a neutral beige, it does not overwhelm. Simplicity, the use of neutral colors, and strong geometry in the artwork around the bed keeps the area from looking cluttered. Traditional sheer curtains filter light into the room.

(opposite) Make the most of a small space through careful decoration. Subtle light-blue-and-white vertical striped wallpaper and framed pictures along with a skirted porcelain sink infuse this tiny pied-a-terre bathroom with an ironic sense of country charm. A small ebony straight-backed chair and a blue-and-white porcelain jardiniere add color to the predominately all-white space.

(above) A newly constructed oversized window frames sunny views of the city and opens up this would-be cramped space. Sculptural hand-forged black iron sconces on either side of the bed help illuminate the room.

(opposite top) Create a light airy guest room with just a few creature comforts in a small apartment. A wrought-iron daybed pushed against the wall doubles as a place to sleep or sit. A metal folding table and a black wrought-iron chair, probably family castoffs, serve as a writing or reading spot. A wall of black and white photographs add interest and dimension to the room.

(opposite middle) A single design element can turn a mundane narrow space into something visually appealing as well as pragmatic. This curved wood chair provides a delightful design element in this bedroom as well as a place for one to sit down to put on their shoes.

(opposite bottom) An Eames-style straight-legged table at the foot of the bed is an element that makes a room both glamorous and functional. Place extra blankets or books on the table. It can also hold a rattan and glass tray stacked with goodies such as coffee, fresh fruit, and crossiants for a pleasant Sunday morning breakfast in bed.

A single design element can turn a mundane narrow space into something virtually appealing....

A curtain divides this small apartment into different spaces. Area rugs in complementary colors of crimson and burnt orange further delineate the space. Compatible styles of furniture, textures of fabrics, and colors create unity.

(right) Sport a witty juxtaposition of dark and light woods and furniture reflective of today and the past to transform a little space into a work of art. This room does both in its design as well as in its choice of art. A profusion of white pillows covers a contemporary dark Indian print sofa adjacent to a white wicker chair under a desk. A 1950s lamp serves as an artistic light source. The photograph hanging above also reflects the mixing and matching of styles–a contemporary home with a vintage convertible Cadillac parked in front.

(opposite) Weave an extra private sleeping, resting or reading nook into an apartment's design with a window seat-*cum*-bed by placing pillows and a mattress on top. A curtain may be pulled across for privacy if the other bed in the room, which doubles as a sofa when entertaining guests, is occupied. For a spark of color, cover the sofa with a multicolored spread of blue, yellow and red to match the color of the walls and palette used in adjoining rooms. Two small wood tables serve as places to position various accessories.

(inset) Soldier blue, mustard yellow, dark red and orange hues offer a contemporary feel to a room, yet they create a sense of peace and place. White on the ceiling makes the room look larger. The living room, library and dining room combination features book shelves for CDs, wine and other collections with space above to place a sculpture or two. Two contemporary wood and metal open-backed chairs placed parallel to a cushioned wicker easy chair offer extra seating near a dining table that doubles as a library table.

Continue a design in contrasts of contemporary and traditional elements. Create the room's canvas with mustard yellow walls. Add a modern European neutral padded sofa, a glass-topped pedestal coffee table, two old-fashioned hand-me-down natural-colored wicker chairs with plush white cushions, then place everything atop a fiery crimson and orange rug. For more drama: Bring out the color of the walls in a blanket tossed ever so casually over the sofa.

(above left) If the apartment has good bones, go with it. Restain a once- dark oak floor, paint walls and moldings, change countertops. Play up soaring uncurtained windows to lighten, brighten and add drama to a small apartment's dining area and kitchen. The use of glass-fronted, unadorned cabinets allows light to filter through, opening up the space.

(above right) Clearly a smaller apartment with a doll-like scale cannot handle imposing antiques but this one features an eclectic mix of good scaled-down pieces set atop a patterned rug. With space at a premium, some furniture must shift gears. A Parson's table can serve as a place to pay bills, read, plan a garden, and with a quick change, the table can be a dining spot or craft center.

(opposite) Do more than push around furniture to make a snug area feel spacious. It's a matter of refining space to achieve a well-made room. For example, enhance the space by enlarging the opening between living room and bedroom. The passage provides not only a striking architectural feature, but separates this apartment's public and private areas. Floor-to-ceiling bookshelves levitating up the walls open up the room while at the same time the hardwood floor topped by an area rug pulls it together.

apartmentalize

Bringing the Outdoors In

Invite nature in and expand the sense of space in your apartment by taking full advantage of views, natural light, and air. The smartest designs marry the apartment and its setting through giant windows left uncovered, skylights, and nooks and crannies where window seats can be built in to savor the vistas. Consider stenciling a floral border around the portal of the interior space that leads to the outdoors. This creates a framing effect and draws the eye to the outside. You don't have much room to be creative, so stick with these small but savvy moves.

Soften the transition from the interior to the openness of the outdoors by *planting flower and herb window boxes at your windows—inside*. Make a list of which plants and colors of each you want so the plants mesh well with the furnishings and surroundings.

If the windowed area that leads to a small, outdoor haven is a kitchen or dining area, be playful. Instead of using traditional indoor furnishings here, *opt for a patio set*. That way, you can still have the pleasure of dining al fresco without ever having to leave the house—perfect for cool evenings or rainy days.

Leave window frames bare of treatments to keep the flow between outdoors and indoors constant. If privacy is an issue, forego heavy draperies, and attach trim screens of vellum or frosted plastic over the lower window sash.

loft spaces

A LOFT APARTMENT presents a special spatial challenge. Whether a vintage example or a new facsimile, it typically represents a cavernous, one-room space that can go on like a run-on sentence that begs for proper punctuation.

In less than fifty years, the loft has metamorphosed from a large, open, gritty, and affordable urban environment with up to 2,000 square feet, 13-foot-high, or higher, ceilings, and light soaring through giant factory windows into a fashionable, streamlined, and often expensive apartment not limited to city environs and certainly not restricted to the less-desirable neighborhoods where they were originally found.

Loft Living

Most lofts still offer a bit of the feeling of living on the edge due to their original use as factories located in industrial neighborhoods. But in many cases, the latest examples have all the trappings of the most sophisticated uptown apartments, including walls, fancy floors and ceilings, shared lobbies, enclosed garages, and even balconies and roofdecks.

Instead of the original occupants—struggling artists, architects, and other professionals who had to work from their homes for economic reasons—the newest crop of owners are successful executives, physicians, lawyers, television and film actors, restaurateurs, writers, and others who have come to see the charm and wisdom of such large-scaled units in interesting neighborhoods.

Residents are also no longer restricted to living in lofts just in downtown New York, where the genre first developed in the large cast-iron manufacturing and printing buildings of the SoHo district, the area south of Houston Street. Over time, the loft concept has spread to more of Manhattan and on to other cities in the U.S. and around the globe. Rather than share a geographic commonality, the tie that binds most lofts is a building that makes economic and aesthetic sense to save and remodel as the back-to-the-city movement continues to grow. More and more people want to avoid commuting, traffic, and copycat suburban residences. And they want to take advantage of all the amenities of city life.

(left and right) Giant roll-down shades shield big slanted windows from strong sunlight and curious nearby occupants in this loft space. An open, metal stairway offers the panache of sleek contemporary design, while at the same time is industrial and cutting edge. Soft leather upholstery tempers the hard-edge decor.

(opposite) Figuring out how much rawness to retain in a loft space usually becomes a balancing act between being true to the original building's purpose and the inhabitant's comfort level and aesthetic preferences. In this space, preserved columns do double duty: they expose the original structure's underskin and they help divide areas visually.

A Loft Apartment for any Style or Preference

With greater acceptance among the mainstream, the interior architecture of lofts has also changed. The loft has evolved from the original "hard" design, so termed because of its hard surfaces, to a "softer" style. The original wood or concrete floors are sometimes covered; the brick or concrete walls are sometimes drywalled; the ceiling ducts, sprinkler systems and timber beams are often concealed; and the walls and halfwalls used to partition off bathrooms sometimes shield bedrooms from the public living spaces as well. Whether these changes are favorable or too far removed from the original form is argued among purists, but many observers of the changes applaud the quieter, more energy efficient and human-oriented lofts that often result.

The way lofts are furnished has also undergone a marked change through the decades. The first generation of lofts tended to be decorated in Salvation Army chic and recycled, second-hand or hand-me-down objects and lacked any thought-out design.

(right) Retain some of the loft feeling by keeping floors, even if they're not the original concrete or wood ones, partly uncovered, the ceilings soaring free, and the furniture arrangements uncrowded. Clever storage–built-in where possible–tends to be limited. Some lofts tend to be dark. White walls and track lighting brighten the space, particularly on cloudy and rainy days.

New Developments

Loft interiors have evolved through the decades, revealing a much wider range of furnishings and styles from the sleekly modern Italian mode, where less still remains more, to the traditional international mix with English or French antiques, American quilts, and Oriental accessories and carpets. The finished design does not look over-manipulated or untouchable, but is relaxed and easy to live in. The most favored look, however, remains a highly edited leanness of whatever period, so that the open feeling associated with this style of apartment comes through strongly. Some call this an undesign—where the unalterable can serve as inspiration.

Two surprising twists in recent loft development are also noteworthy and bode well for future occupants who desire a choice. Brand-new lofts are now built to mimic the original buildings, but these modern architectural versions are made with a combination of both old-fashioned attention to the art of the structure and new amenities. In addition, the boundaries of acceptable areas in which to live in a loft have been expanded to the suburbs and ex-urban areas, so now more can enjoy the form. The primary goal of the loft, however, remains the same: a surfeit of space, light, and air and an eclectic exuberance in the choice of furnishings and accessories.

(opposite) clockwise from top left:

A partial wall and glass screen provide the only barrier to the bedroom area of this loft space.

Furniture can be arranged and rearranged in a loft—it's one of the luxuries of living in a wide-open space. Keep furnishings away from walls to highlight openness and don't overcrowd. Rest artworks on the floor against the wall as an alternative to hanging. This adds an intimacy to the quarters rather than focusing on the vastness of the walls and square footage.

Metal-framed modern furnishings are at home in loft spaces since the frames echo the hard-edged rawness of the original spaces. Contemporary furniture suits this setting, particularly when used sparingly and with few accessories against a pickled hardwood floor.

Try a minimalist approach in your loft space. Keep the palette monochromatic with pale wood floors, all white walls, uncurtained windows, and ribbed glass screens/doors to offer a hint of room divisions.

apartmentalize

Tips on Designing a Loft Space

Through the years, as more loft residents have had the money to decorate, they have helped spawn a loft aesthetic, which usually depended on industrial steel shelves, restaurant equipment, rubber matting and gym-style lockers, to cite just a few of the style's favorite accoutrements. These looked right at home amid the brick or cinder block walls, the wood or concrete floors, and the exposed ceilings with their piping stretching across huge expanses. But, as the look has become more finished, the furnishings, too, have softened, and now almost anything goes. You might keep the areas bright and cheerful with light, paint, and fabrics. Lively colors that vary in intensity can also provide a unifying design statement and visual harmony from area to area. Here are some ideas to guide you, no matter what type of loft you favor.

Retain some of the original charm.
Whether it is exposed-brick walls or concrete floors or stairs to a second level. Let the large factory windows remain in view rather than camouflage them with traditional curtains.

Strive for a *mix of styles*; do not make everything match. Bring out those flea-market finds and mix and match them with more upscale items. Use different chairs around a kitchen or dining room table rather than a matched set.

Add a row or two of *sleek track lighting* rather than lots of small lamps. Install a ceiling fan with a light kit or a halogen lamp for illumination. If a loft is too dark to begin with, you can lighten and brighten it with some white paint or various shades of white on the ceiling or a wall or two.

Just because lofts don't have as many walls and doors as more traditional apartments doesn't mean that occupants need to give up any creature comforts such as TVs, books and pleasurable seating. Scale helps make the look work. Furniture should not be too small and demure to fit the cavernous spaces. Warm woods and leathers soften one loft's minimalism.

(above) Some of the best-designed lofts reflect a playfulness that suggests the owners haven't forgotten the former manifestation of the quarters. Case in point: the bicycle wheels supporting this glass table make it look like it might take off for the Tour de France at a moment's notice.

(right) The spare loft aesthetic was replaced with a more traditional environment in this space. A glass coffee table stacked with books, groupings of framed artworks, and furniture arranged around the table for intimate conversation creates a homey feel.

(opposite) Anything goes in a loft, from the highly designed to the barely adorned. The space need not reflect all minimalism and contemporary elan. Sunny yellow walls, a black window shade, wooden furniture and a comfortable old-style coverlet set forth an undecorated look.

(left) A loose gathering of modern and antique furnishings conveys relaxed glamour in this generously sized apartment. Large apartments allow you to do two things at once: Display a collection of photography and create an art gallery along a large, empty wall of your living room. Chic detail: Use frames of only slightly different thickness and color to keep the display stylishly simple.

(below) Free-standing shelves hold precious collections and make superb room dividers in both large and small apartments. A prized collection of pottery is displayed in a custom-designed storage unit—the grid pattern of the shelves helps to break up the large proportions of the unit.

(previous page) The first lofts usually housed artists and their studios. This particular one retains that feeling with its wall of framed art-works in stacked gallery fashion and large canvases hung with room to breathe. When the walls are crowded, keep the furnishings simple. Here, a large table of wood echoes the columns, adding an aged patina that contrasts well with all the whiteness and newness.

(opposite) clockwise from top left:

Closets blend right into the walls of this hallway. The storage they provide allow the space to remain clean and spare.

One shot of surprising color in the form of hot yellow curtains livens up this clean-lined loft where classic modern furnishings such as an Eames chair surround a glass-topped coffee table. A stainless steel floor lamp and one elegant vase filled with fresh blooms serve as the only accessories.

One curved wall left unadorned makes a bold statement in a streamlined loft of white walls and pale wood floors. Built-in shelves at the far end provide needed storage and display space since many lofts have minimal closets. Prepare walls well before painting white since imperfections will stand out even more when surfaces are so crisp and clean.

Shiny new floorboards, protected with several coats of a sealer, make uncarpeted floors practical and also allow furniture to be quickly rearranged and extra tables brought in for large parties. When the lines of the loft are architecturally interesting, there's no need to cover windows with curtains; let the views and light stream in instead.

(opposite) Since the walls of this space are white, the riot of color expressed by the furnishings, ranging from buttery yellow chairs to a red ottoman, purple sofa, and blue end table, adds a sense of fun. The colorful area rug ties it all together.

(above) Glass shelves provide a whimsical
way to display glassware in the kitchen area
of a loft space. The see-through quality helps
keep the look spare while providing storage.

(opposite) The kitchen in this loft retains its
urban openness, but has a fresh clean-lined
appearance with white cabinetry and countertops, simple display shelves and big windows that allow in light. The colorful strips of
the wooden floor add an unusual panache.

(page 78) Flexible furniture has become more in vogue in recent years. In this apartment, the nightstand on wheels might be rolled out to the living area to serve as a coffee table or end table. The bed is also on wheels so it's easy enough to relocate the sleeping quarters when the need is felt. And although they have the look of built-ins, the bookshelves are readily dismantled.

(page 79) A patchwork quilt and colored wooden strips across the floor repeat the blues, yellows and other hues used elsewhere in the space.

(opposite) Closets concealed by opaque doors are likely to become disorganized, but that's seldom the case when what's stored in a closet is visible behind frosted glass doors. In keeping with the openness aesthetic of the loft, this closet is actually not entirely closed off.

apartmentalize

Keeping It Open When decorating your loft, remember its original legacy of openness, even if yours is somewhat closed off with walls, doors and softer materials. Do not divide the space into tiny cubicles, but plan your loft space with wide-open, interlinked areas. You might use large-sized furniture pieces rather than small ones that will prove distracting—and don't feel compelled to fill every corner and nook. Or create smaller sitting or work areas within the expansiveness through area rugs or a change in the flooring material. To enjoy the open and airy feeling of loft living, and to make your apartment as functional as possible, follow these tips.

Keep all the *furniture in the middle of the space* so there's plenty of room to move about the perimeter.

Try dividing the space. Employ *screens, sleek doors, or a wall of books*, but make sure none of these goes all the way to the ceiling.

Add various "rooms" in your loft space by *arranging chairs in "conversation areas"* around the space.

chic
apartments

AROUND THE GLOBE, in New York, Honolulu, Hong Kong, and Tokyo, sprawling, stunning, chic apartments dot cosmopolitan landscapes. These residences seem larger than life and are coveted and appraised like expensive jewels. Many of these highly chic apartments are the homes of professional designers and artists—those with a strong sense of just how something should look and how to set a mood with style.

Apartment Chic   Chic apartments take on many styles and forms. They might be decorated in high-style Victorian or in clean, minimalist themes. They might even be arrayed in an eclectic cacophony of styles in which antique pieces are artfully displayed in a sea of modernism. One thing's for sure about these kinds of apartments: each has a style all its own. Whether large or small, divided by rooms or wide-open spaces, you know when you've walked into one of these gems. Your reaction is to stop, look around, and soak in every piece, every detail.

Creating a chic apartment is reliant on many factors. Exquisite taste and an eye for one-of-a-kind pieces is part of it, but a sense of architectural form and detail can play a huge role in how your chic apartment evolves. The space itself is as important as the pieces you bring to it so the first step is to find just the right shell in which to show off your treasures. Whether you choose an older building replete with architectural charm of its own or a glass box in a modern skyscraper, this will set the backdrop for how the rest of the design evolves.

(above) If a room is not big enough for a canopy bed, improvise. Here, a valance with billowing curtains tacked on the wall appears to almost envelop the bed, which is pushed right up against the wall for effect. The plant becomes a canopy in and of itself as it drapes over the bed.

(following spread) If space permits, set up more than on seating group in your living room. Unify the scheme with color, style, or perhaps a shared item like a rug or ottoman. Be sure that symmetry doesn't rule, however. In chic apartments, rooms should feature some unevenness for drama.

Creating Your Own Sense of Chic

In some cases, units in vintage buildings have retained their luxury of space and also preserved their architectural charm. Details, such as moldings and carved ceilings, abound in such apartments. These spaces can be desirable, but the downside is that some of them may have been ignored or altered unfavorably through the years, thereby requiring a great deal of time and money to bring their structure and design back to life. They may also require excessive work and funds to maintain them in their improved state.

There are many questions you should be asking yourself before selecting an apartment. Do you want to rent or buy, and based on this, how much money do you want to spend? Are you willing to forgo some of the ultra-modern conveniences like a deluxe shower system that an older building might not be able to accommodate—or are you willing to live in a uniform space without any architectural charm? And if it's a matter of simply redecorating your present residence, can you work with the existing architectural style to create the chic apartment of your dreams?

Once you've selected your shell, it's time to start decorating. In a chic apartment, hardwood floors adorned by elegant area rugs to designate room areas are common, but so are spaces covered in plush, thick, wall-to-wall carpeting. There is no one floor-covering standard in determining what makes an apartment "chic," so there's no one way to decorate it either.

(opposite) Large dining rooms are not de rigueur; in fact, the smaller the area the more intimate for a chic tête-à-tête at home. Even a card table covered in a pretty printed fabric with two interesting side or armchairs can create a proper dining spot—bon appetit!

(left) If a kitchen unfolds within view of the dining area, get creative and add some printed fabric to hide cabinets, an oven and utensils such as extra pots and pans. Chic apartment living means skillfully mixing different prints and styles; a Chinese-style lantern adds whimsy in an otherwise Continental-style setting.

A traditional style sectional with big roll
arms and thick pillows fits into its snug corner, inviting conversation, reading, and
dreaming. Pattern comes in through the
Chinese-inspired area rug. The mirror over
the fireplace reflects the books on the
shelves of the opposite wall, creating the
effect of a painting.

Setting The Mood

The decisions you make about wall coverings will set the mood in your apartment. Will it be serious and austere, or warm and elegant? Do you want to introduce a lot of pattern on the walls and then select more subdued furniture pieces, or do you want the walls to serve as a backdrop for what you bring in? Certainly some might say that the walls should be the backdrop and that's all, but what if you decide to cover the wall in an exciting hand-painted mural that spans floor to ceiling, or inlay a mosaic pattern in one of the walls? The point is that there are times when the walls themselves can be focal points so you must decide carefully on how they will look and what kind of statement they will make in your chic apartment.

Furniture selections should be taken very seriously. No matter what kind of apartment you live in, your furniture is a natural focal point. In a chic apartment, furniture can mean the difference between chic and gauche. The same holds true for accessories. Depending on how interesting or eye-catching these pieces are, finishing touches like an antique vase or a carefully placed lamp can take attention away from prominent furniture pieces and become focal points in and of themselves.

A curtain suspended from the ceiling along a stairway can cordon off the upstairs and create a sense of mystery for what lies beyond. In this apartment, the off-white fabric adds color and texture, particularly on the uncarpeted stairwell, covered at the bottom with an off-white and burgundy striped linen runner.

(opposite) Using multiple hues from the same color family is an art form. In this airy bedroom, the different blues used on an armchair, bed linens, coverlet, walls, and windows speak elegantly but are hardly monotonously. Contrasts come from the wooden floor and framed artworks, grouped for emphasis.

But how you decorate a chic apartment need not be all on the inside. If you have a view, it can become part of the design. Flaunt it to make the room and your apartment look larger. Balconies, patios, roofdecks, bay windows, and window seats offer private places and make an apartment seem larger and cheerier because of the light and outdoor vistas they reveal. A nature-scape or cityscape will create different moods in a design scheme. Think carefully about whether or not your particular view will enhance your décor or detract from it before you bring the outdoors in.

The most important consideration for decorating a chic apartment is to not let form overcome function. Remember, this is not a museum piece, it is where you live. No matter what means you take to make it a showpiece, don't forget that you have to exist there everyday. Consider what that means in terms of what goes on in your life on a daily basis, but don't forget the most crucial concept: comfort. No matter how intriguing your apartment looks, it still must be a space in which you can put your feet up and really call it home.

(left) This garret-style bedroom has been elegantly furnished with period trappings: flowing curtains, a cushioned window seat, rows of pillows, and favorite artworks. A chair does double duty as a host for a breakfast tray and tea-time snacks as well as a place to sit.

(opposite) The epitome of luxury in a bathroom is a fireplace, particularly on cold winter days. An antique claw-footed tub completes the luxurious effect. A tub like this can probably be found at a salvage shop. A shower curtain hung from the ceiling provides privacy.

(above) Gravel forms a natural floor covering in the courtyard of an apartment in an 1840s townhouse. A perimeter of green becomes low-maintenance even for those with less than green thumbs. Keep furniture all-weather so it can be left outside in any type of weather.

(opposite) A charming enhancement to a chic bathroom, this original pedestal sink was restored using new brass polishing for its legs and fittings. A new crisp white-tiled floor, canary yellow walls, deeper yellow curtains, and fluffy white towels freshen up the bathroom and make it welcoming and stylish.

apartmentalize

Make an Ordinary Space Extraordinary: Add Chic to the Rooms in Your Apartment

To make an ordinary apartment into a chic space, you don't necessarily need a lot of money. As is true in all interior design plans, a little ingenuity and creativity goes a long way. Consider concocting a shower unit from aluminum window frames instead of more expensive glass blocks, or, make railings, which can also be dividers, from standard-issue copper or aluminum piping or tubing. Here are some more tips for turning functional into fabulous.

Substitute *gauzy nylon* for silk swags at windows or to drape a four-poster bed.

Include *flea-market finds, architectural artifacts, or folk-art heirlooms* for that extra dimension. Grouped with modern furnishings or as an eclectic mix, the effect can be glamorous and comfortable, yet not overdone.

Play up details for decorative impact. Carefully choose your doorknobs, coat hooks, and drawer handles with an eye toward lively color and unusual shapes and materials. Interesting lampshades with embroidery, piping, scalloping, pleating, and hand painting also add pattern, color, and texture.

(top) Massive wooden doors accented by large round medallions and installed in the original doorway reveal an elegant sitting room beyond, where family treasures abound in the form of artworks, books, and mementos.

(bottom) Arrange furniture in the center of a room where the architectural elements of floors, walls, windows, and moldings serve as part of the decor. A central furniture arrangement, anchored here by a rug, also creates a cozy intimacy within an expansive chic space.

(opposite) Don't camouflage beautiful old windows and moldings with layers of curtains or other window treatments when the original bones are sufficient to produce that ìwowî effect. The only exception should be if the view is an eyesore.

(opposite, top left) An unusual collection of metal shapes makes for an eye-catching display and stands out against the celadon painted walls.

(opposite, top right) Use height as a decorative device in an apartment where tall space should be accentuated. Emphasize it using color, window treatments, and tall objects such as candelabra, rows of books, and artwork and mirrors hung one above the other.

(opposite, bottom) Some of the smartest chic apartments do not feel like they have been decorated all. Incorporate furniture and accessories from different periods and with varied fabrics and textures to achieve that look.

(right) Chic apartments don't follow tried-and-true decorating rules. For example, separate a pair of artworks on either side of a much larger piece rather than hang them together. Upholster furnishings in different fabrics but use those that share a common denominator of a hue, texture, or scale. Unify the elements through one major link—in this case an area rug.

Chic doesn't necessarily mean luxurious,
rather it's a reflection of attitude. Some chic
rooms do double duty, such as living spaces,
dining spaces or work areas. The secret of
multipurpose success: carve out places to
stash papers and dishes when the other
functions are called into action.

(left) One great decorative accessory, in this case an old crystal chandelier festooned with detailing, can become the only necessary focal point in chic living space. Your best bet: shop less traditional venues such as flea markets and the Internet.

(right) Angle one piece of furniture against a corner for visual interest. Although symmetry can sometimes prove boring and ho-hum, a great pair of anything—such as lamps—proves that every decorating rule has exceptions, particularly when placing something dramatic in between.

A cacaphony of style. In this chic living room, sectionals are upholstered in purple, the Louis XV armchairs in hot pink, and the custom-made roundabout in an animal print, so the total effect dazzles the eye. White walls allow the individual pieces to stand out.

(above) Unsure how to hang art and photographs in an attractive grouping? Consider bringing in an art installer who knows just how to arrange small and larger works together without pounding unnecessary nail holes into freshly painted walls.

(opposite) An antique chair has a whole new life when upholstered in wild pink, purple, green, and blue silk fabric, complemented by a lampshade of a similar apple-green hue.

(opposite) A dash of shocking color and pattern bring to life a traditional bedroom that remains chic since both the color and pattern are modest in the scheme of the entire room. The headboard wears a deep pink while the bench sports a rainbow-colored patterned fabric. An antique screen, chaise, and night stands reveal a respect for tradition.

(above) True chic equates as much with comfort as luxury. This silk-upholstered neo-rococo chaise lounge occupies an important corner with a good reading light, a night stand and side table for papers, books, and a glass of wine. The mirror doubles the beauty and the space; the Vertes screen acts as a visual backdrop.

apartmentalize

Natural Chic How can you create a garden space in your chic apartment —even if you don't have an outdoor living space? It's easier than you think. For instance, create an indoor "patio." Use laid back, comfortably upholstered furniture in your living room, such as faded florals or sun-washed checks and plaids. Cushions and pillows work well to bring the outdoors in and a sisal area rug can add a nice touch. Follow these tips to create relaxing garden retreats within your home.

Repeat a *garden-like motif* throughout your apartment. Use materials such as wrought-iron or twig furniture in tables, chairs, chaises, settees, plant stands, and stools.

In the kitchen, *favorite collectibles* that give the feeling of being at a picnic on a summer's day, such as Fiestaware, can lead the color scheme.

Pottery is at home in all settings and will create the feeling of a garden space when used artfully in your home. A large terra-cotta pot can be used as a divider, an object d'art, or as a container for fruit, flowers, or herbs. Use creative containers such as jelly jars, a collection of hoop-handled baskets filled with bursts of color such as a grouping of lemons or limes, vintage ceramic pots and jardinieres, or old watering cans for the same effect.

living large

IT'S WHAT SO many of us long for—living space as far as the eye can see. Lots of walls for hanging art. Glorious windows everywhere for capitalizing on natural light. More storage space than we ever dreamed possible. Even though oversized apartments provide a wealth of room for living, however, they still present their share of design challenges.

Planning a Large Space

How can you create a sense of intimacy, hominess, coziness in such an immense space? If you recruit an interior designer, how can you be sure that for every inch of your apartment that the personality coming across is yours and not that of the decorator or an architect? And with all that space to fill, should you acquire furnishings quickly so that you can't hear your own voice echoing in the emptiness, or should you be patient and gradually decorate as you find the right furnishings and accessories? Are we just grasping at straws trying to pinpoint what's not great about a large apartment? Probably a little bit.

The fact is that sizable, roomy apartments provide one of the most desirable and comfortable living situations. You are free to keep your space as spare as you like or to accumulate at whim. Do you have room for that adorable little Victorian bench you saw at the antique show? Of course you do. There's always room. Studio apartment and other small apartment dwellers envy you as they know they can only desire such treasures from afar—they're sometimes lucky just to fit a couch and a bed in their apartments.

(left) Spontaneity in design abounds in this spacious New York City apartment. Owners breathed new life into the square footage by playing with color and mixing antiques and flea market finds. A few fine pieces cost serious money like the classic cushioned sofa in this study. For contrast, a brown and beige striped afghan tossed over the arm of the sofa softens brighter colors, as do several throw pillows. Everything has its place such as family photos that run up and down the walls.

An enormous living room provides space for a comfortable seating arrangement as well as a homework area. Authentic English antiques combine with flea-market treasures. Striped handmade curtains hang above a dyed pink calico sofa. A hodgepodge of reupholstered armchairs in mismatched chintz and stripes create a playful, very English air. The room effervesces in pastels of pink, blue, yellow, green, and a primary red. Furniture sits atop a Saruk Oriental to pull the space together.

And that's not the only upside of larger apartments. Consider the freedom a large apartment gives. What do you do with all that space? If you have a family, you might just have enough room for everyone to have their own "space," which could mean bedroom, but depending on how large the apartment is, it could mean a whole lot more.

For example, do you find yourself taking work home from the office at night or on weekends? If so, where do you work? In a large apartment, you might be able to set aside an entire room of your own—or even a corner or nook—that you can transform into an office for yourself. What about hobbyists? Every household has its share of these. Why not eke out a special place for that hobby to be performed. Perhaps you have several small children and all the requisite toys that go along with them. A playroom or play area designated by a colorful rug and a toy box is also a strong possibility in a large apartment.

Another thing you'll enjoy in a large apartment is the freedom to break out of the confines of traditional decorating. You can trick the eye with clever furniture placement. Float a sofa with a table set behind it, or place the sofa diagonally against the corner. In a small apartment, you'd be asking for trouble with either of these solutions because they can eat up too much space. However, in a large apartment, you have the freedom to try out unusual furniture placements. Take advantage of it.

(left) Dazzling color and cleverness dictate the look in a boy's bathroom in a large apartment. The white pedestal sink creates a venerable European flavor, while the sea green and white checked pattern of the floor picks up the pattern of curtains in adjoining rooms. In lieu of a linen closet, an English campaign chest stores linens.

(opposite) The bedroom of every little girl's dreams. When a room is big enough, possessions can create personality and not clutter. While the white canopied bed is the room's focal point, the enormous window with its sea green and white gingham curtains makes for a close second.

Keeping a Cohesive Space

Of course, large apartments do have their downsides. One of these lies in creating a sense of cohesiveness in the big space. Whether the apartment is older or brand new, a sense of unity in the decoration is always desirable in an apartment—large or small. In a house, there's usually room to depart from the mood of the general design on different floors—not to mention attics and basements—but an apartment is usually taken in all at once, no matter how large it is.

The smartest design professionals and apartment owners recommend that you consider the whole space when designing any one room or section in the apartment. If you're just moving in, you might live in your apartment for a while to get a sense of the space before you call in the decorators. If you're redecorating the apartment you've been living in for years, start looking at the space as objectively as you can, analyzing what really works designwise and what—and be honest—has never worked. While the rooms of your apartment need not appear as though finished in one fell swoop with one repetitive style, the goal should be to aim for a coherent background decor and compatible palette.

(opposite) Pastels contrast with a palette of reds and yellows in the kitchen of a large apartment to give the room visual interest as well as a distinct coziness despite the vastness of the space. The room combines old furniture and junkyard finds with brand new pieces. Still life paintings add a touch of tradition to the walls.

Valentine's Day red spray-painted cabinets dominate this eclectic kitchen in a large apartment. The black-and-white checked floor adds dimension and sparkle. Floral print cafÈ curtains with red and white striped valance and matching fabric on an iron soda fountain chair in an antique black finish all vie for the spotlight.

(opposite) When there's room to accommodate it, an enormous nineteenth-century
French Provencal chair holds its own next to
a fringe-skirted bed in this tremendous master suite. Raspberry and white stripes on a
fabric-covered headboard, raspberry-painted
walls and a settee with fabric matching the
headboard creates a European ambience.

For many residents of enormous apartments, decorating can ultimately become an issue of what to leave out rather than what to include. Having surplus room gives you the luxury of following design formulas only if you want to. You can transform an enormous foyer into an art gallery as well as a welcoming space. An oversized dining room can become a library at one end. Former servants' quarters become excellent teenager's hangouts or guest bedrooms. Or, you can enjoy your enormous space in the purest state— left bare and uncluttered to savor its grandeur and scope.

(above) Storage comes in unexpected places. A once blank wall above built-in cabinets near the kitchen make the perfect spot for shelving in a large apartment. Clever recycling results in a free-floating hand-painted shelf, formerly a desk hutch with a drawer. It comes to life again in this kitchen as a container for ceramics, cookbooks, and topiaries.

(opposite) A mish-mash of old and new woods and colors energizes this large kitchen. Glass-fronted cabinetsóone painted blue-green and the other sunny yellowópro-vide storage for everyday dishes and glassware. Rounded painted shelves hold books, plates, and plants adding detail, warmth and chic.

(above) A single design element adds a clever conversation piece to a room. Rescue an old safe and transform it into a charming place for storing and hiding mundane items or good china. Paint old shutters and use in lieu of doors to create another clever storage spot to hang clothes that are out of season. Recycled shutters can also double as great room dividers in this large apartment.

(right) Even in gigantic apartments, storage can be insufficient. Merge old technology and design to create more storage and make a clever statement at the same time. An old refurbished icebox conceals kitchen supplies. When a kitchen becomes a family gathering place, move cushy pieces into the room such as a comfortable bench.

apartmentalize

Planning Is Everything

Ironically, sometimes those who live in large apartments use their spaces less efficiently than those who live in smaller apartments. The reason? In smaller spaces, necessity becomes the mother of inventiveness. If you want to hold on to anything, you have to be clever about where to keep it so that it's not in the way. But when you don't use your space wisely and efficiently in a large space, it shows. In any apartment situation where possessions are not properly stored, it will look like a storm just blew through. And if you have too much stuff, it could give you and your guests a headache trying to take it all in. Most importantly in the case of a large apartment, how will you ever expect to find anything if you don't have a sense of order and organization?

Do not fill every nook and cranny with stuff. Give each piece of furniture or built-in enough room to really stand out.

How can you make the most of any space you live in? The following tips will inspire you in the ways of making a large apartment a luxurious yet livable space.

Don't let the accumulated spoils of your life crowd you out of apartment and home. *There's a place for everything and everything in its place*— so find it and put it away. Get into the habit of sifting through and tossing accumulated mail, books, magazines, and all the detritus of life that builds up over time.

Tuck away storage containers in closets.
Roll low-lying storage under beds; leave the ubiquitous armoire in a prominent spot and conceal within it a television, stereo, and other odds and ends to keep an entire wall or two free for that appealing, uncluttered look.

(previous page) Carve out a series of lively contours in a large living room. A contemporary floor lamp with cylinder-shaped shade peers over a long beige leather sofa, curvaceous and asymmetrical Eames-style wood and metal coffee table, buttery yellow metal and wood basket weave chair and a stuffed armless wing chair.

A sparingly furnished dining room in a large apartment offers diners views of the living room (featured, left) and the predominately stainless steel kitchen. A contemporary wood buffet with white Formica top acts as a twin to the long dining room table as well as a perfect repository for a bit of greenery. The uncarpeted hardwood floor adds to the definite starkness of the room that adheres to the Mies van der Rohe philosophy of design that less is more. A quartet of contemporary prints adds a trace of color.

(above) It takes a large dining room in a large apartment to handle a synthesis of periods and styles. The straight-legged long wood dining table and eight-curvaceous dining chairs whose design harks back to the 1950s, resembles a minimalist sculpture. The design combines the comfort of handmade pieces to blunt the sharpness of cutting-edge technology.

(opposite) A contemporary ambience in the dining area of this large apartment flows into the kitchen where the use of stainless steel, white painted walls, and laminate cabinets provide the visual motif. The stainless steel items reflect the light filtering through a near-by window making the room brighter. Stainless counters and a full-size refrigerator make the kitchen functional with everything within arms reach.

Directory of Photographers

Roland Beaufre
24 Boulevard Barbes
75018 Paris
France
011-33147929610
Fax: 011-33140200652

Fernando Bengoechea
Agenzia Masi
Viale Monza, 48
20127 Milano, Italy
02-2610819
Fax: 02-2826262

Tony Berardi
Photofields
36W830 Stonebridge Lane
St. Charles, IL 60175
(630) 587-5530
Fax: (630)584-8035

Nadia Mackenzie
Interior Archive
15 Grand Union Centre
West Row, London W10 5AS
171-370-0595
Fax: 181-960-2695

Peter Margonelli
20 Desbrosses St.
New York, NY 10013
(212) 941-0380
Fax: (212) 334-4449

Michael Moran
371 Broadway, 2nd Floor
New York, NY 10013
(212) 334-4543
Fax: (212) 343-3854

Tim Street-Porter
2074 Watsonia Terrace
Los Angeles, CA 90068
(323) 874-4278
Fax: (323) 876-8795

Eric Roth
337 Summer St.
Boston, MA 02210
(617) 338-5358
Fax: (617) 338-6098

Dao-Lou Zha
courtesy of
Cha & Innerhofer Architecture + Design
611 Broadway, Suite 540
New York, NY 10012
(212) 477-6957
fax: (212) 353-3286

Photo Credits

Roland Beaufre 23, 38, 39, 59, 102, 103, 104, 105, 106, 107, 115, 133

Fernando Bengoechea 7, 10, 12, 16, 17, 18, 19, 20, 21, 24, 25, 26, 28, 30, 31, 32, 33, 39, 49, 60, 61, 67, 68, 69, 70, 75, 76, 77, 78, 79, 81, 84, 86, 87, 88, 89, 90, 91, 92, 94, 95, 96, 97, 98, 99, 100, 101, 108, 110, 111, 112, 113, 114, 115, 116, 118, 120, 122, 123, 124, 125, 127, 132, 133

Tony Berardi 11, 73, 82

Nadia Mackenzie, Interior Archive 49

Peter Margonelli 2, 13, 42, 43, 44, 45, 83, 134, 136, 137, 138, 139

Michael Moran 50, 52, 53, 55, 57, 60,61,82, 83

Tim Street-Porter 34, 35, 37, 62, 64, 65

Eric Roth 128, 129, 130, 131

Dao-Lou Zha 46, 47

ABC Carpet and Home
881 & 888 Broadway at E. 19th Street
New York, NY 10003
(212)-473-3000
www.abchome.com

Aero Furniture
011-44-181-971-0022

Alchemy
(310)-836-8631
www.alchemy-glass.com

Anichini
Route 110
Turnbridge, VT 05077
1-800-553-5309
www.anichini.com

Anthropologie
1700 Sansom Street, 6th Floor
Philadelphia, PA 19103
1-800-309-2500/ 1-800-543-1039
www.anthropologie.com

Bed + Bath
12817 Preston Road, Suite 128
Dallas, TX 75230
within the US only:1-800-945-7714
Outside the US: 1-972-783-9502
www.bedandbath.com

Bed, Bath and Beyond
1-800-GO-BEYOND
www.bedbathandbeyond.com

The Bombay Company
P.O. Box 161009
Fort Worth, TX 76161-1009
1-800-829-7789
www.bombayco.com

Cappellini-Modern Age
102 Wooster Street
New York, NY 10012
(212)-966-0669
www.cappelini.it

The Conran Shop
Michelin House
81 Fulham Road
London SW3 6RD
0171-591-8702
www.conran.co.uk

The Container Store
200 Valwood Parkway
Dallas, TX 75234-8800
1-800-733-3532
www.containerstore.com

Crate & Barrel
www.crateandbarrel.com

Dean and Deluca
2526 East 36th St. North Circle
Wichita, Kansas 67219
1-800-781-4050
www.deandeluca.com

Essential Home
3775 24th Street
San Francisco, CA 94114
1-888-282-3330
www.essentialhome.com

Gardener,s Eden
P.O. Box 7307
San Francisco, CA 94120-7307
1-800-822-9600

Garnet Hill
1-800-622-6216
www.garnethill.com

IKEA
1-800-434-ikea
www.ikea.com

Kitchen Etc...
32 Industrial Drive
Exeter, NH 03833
1-800 232-4070
www.kitchenetc.com

Kmart
1-800-63-KMART
www.bluelight.com

Linen 'n Things
6 Brighton Road
Clifton, NJ 07015
(973)-815-2974
www.linensnthings.com

Luminaire
301 West Superior
Chicago, IL 60610
1-800-494-4358

Ovation
73 Lafayette Street
Marblehead, MA 01945
(781)-639-4754
www.ovationfurniture.com

Pier 1 Imports
461 Fifth Ave
New York, NY 10017
1-800-447-4371
www.pier1.com

Placewares
160 Newbury Street
Boston, MA 02116-2833
(617) 267-5460
www.placewares.com

Pottery Barn
P.O.Box 7044
San Francisco, CA 94120
1-800-922-5507
www.potterybarn.com

Smith + Hawken
1-800-940-1170
www.smithandhawken.com

Spiegel
P.O.Box 182555
Columbus, OH 43218-2555
1-800-474-5555
www.spiegel.com

Takashimaya
693 Fifth Avenue
New York, NY 10022
1-800-753-2038

Target
1-888-304-4000
www.target.com

Urban Archaeology
143 Franklin Street
New York, NY 10013
(212)-431-4646

Urban Outfitters
4040 Locust Street
Philadelphia, PA 19104
(215)-387-0373

Williams-Sonoma
1-800-840-2591
www.williams-sonoma.com

About the Authors

Barbara B. Buchholz and Margaret Crane have co-authored several books, including *Successful Homebuilding and Remodeling: Real-Life Advice for Getting the House You Want Without the Roof (or Sky) Falling In*, *The Family Business Answer Book: Arthur Andersen Tackles 101 of Your toughest Questons*, and *Corporate Bloodlines: The Future of the Family Firm*. Both also write independently; their articles have appeared in the *Chicago Tribune*, *Crain's Chicago Business*, *Midwest Living*, *House Beautiful*, *Chicago Home and Garden*, and the *New York Times*. Both live in houses in St. Louis, Missouri, but they and their families have lived in apartments in New York, Chicago, and St. Louis.

Photos: Andrew R. Newman